GW00731495

Osc.. ......

Archbishop of San Salvador and Martyr

by
Fr Ashley Beck

*All booklets are published thanks to the
generous support of the members of the
Catholic Truth Society*

CATHOLIC TRUTH SOCIETY
PUBLISHERS TO THE HOLY SEE

Contents

Acknowledgements

Many people in England are far better qualified than me to write about Archbishop Romero, and I am grateful to CTS for giving me the privilege of doing so. Among those who have encouraged and supported me are the Bishop of East Anglia, the Rt Rev Michael Evans, and my wife Caroline, who has always had a strong interest in Oscar Romero. I am also grateful to Fr Kevin Doran and Mungo Lockhart, in whose homes in Ireland and Burgundy respectively much of the work for this booklet was done.

Martyr's Witness

In early 2007 Pope Benedict XVI travelled to Latin
America for the first time as pope to open the Fifth
General Assembly of the Council of Bishops of Latin
America (CELAM) at Aparaceida in Brazil. On the
aeroplane he gave an extended interview during which he
gave some reflections about past and future directions in
'Liberation Theology.' He also said this, in answer to a
question about moves to beatify the Servant of God[1]
Oscar Romero, fourth Archbishop of San Salvador, who
was shot while saying Mass on 24th March 1980:

'Archbishop Romero was certainly an important witness
of the faith, a man of great Christian virtue who worked
for peace and against the dictatorship, and was killed
while celebrating Mass. Consequently, his death was
truly "credible", a witness of faith.'[2]

Sainthood

Ten years after Romero's death the Archdiocese of San
Salvador submitted documents for the consideration of
the cause for his beatification and eventual canonisation.
In the countries of Latin America - the small country of

El Salvador and many other places - a popular cult of Oscar Romero developed very quickly and in many places he is already venerated as a saint. Among Catholics, other Christians and many others without religious beliefs he has become an iconic figure in the struggle of the poor and oppressed throughout the world - in countless homes, churches and other places in Latin America his image is to be found as a source of strength for some of the poorest people of the world. Throughout the history of the Church, movements for canonisation often begin at 'grass roots', beginning with the simple faith of the people. It is clear that this is what is happening with Oscar Romero, and this booklet is a contribution to the process of reflection in which the whole Church is engaged in assessing the life and death of Romero. It is also good to reflect again on his importance because 2007 sees the ninetieth anniversary of his birth, but there are three further reasons why this is a good time. The first is the Church's continuing reflection about the importance of martyrdom, centred on our experience of the Jubilee year 2000. Pope John Paul II, in his letter *Tertio Millennio Adveniente* (1994) and elsewhere, called on all of us be aware of the place of martyrs and their 'stories'. He wrote 'The Church has once again become a Church of martyrs.' The pope also wrote in his 1998 encyclical about the relationship between religious faith and philosophy:

'I am thinking first of all of the witness of martyrs. The martyr, in effect, is the most authentic witness to the truth about existence. He knows that he has found in the encounter with Jesus Christ the truth about his life and no one and no thing can ever take away that certainty. Neither suffering nor a violent death will force him to separate from the adherence to truth that he has found in his encounter with Christ. This is why the witness of martyrs is accepted, listened to, and followed even in our day. It is the reason why trust their word; we perceive in them the evidence of a love that has no need of long arguments to be convinced, since it speaks to each person of what they already perceive internally as true and long-sought-after. Certainly, the martyr produces great confidence in ourselves, because he articulates what we already feel, and he makes evident what we would also like to have the strength to express.'[3]

Romero's true place

John Paul II also stresses that the phenomenon of martyrdom has brought Christians from different traditions and backgrounds closer together: the new Archbishop Romero Trust in Britain is a good example of this, and a statue of Romero was erected above the west door of Westminster Abbey, with images of other modern martyrs, in 1998.[4]

The second reason why it is a good time to refresh our awareness of Romero's importance is that one theological concept important for him, the notion of the 'preferential option for the poor' has become far more at the centre of Catholic life than would have been true at the time of his death - perhaps partly because of his death. It is not simply now an idea associated with the 'theologies of liberation' but rather something which is 'mainstream' and part of the Church's whole body of authoritative teaching.[5] Along with important developments in the theologies of liberation, what this means is that much of the message of Romero is much less controversial among Catholics than would have been the case a quarter of a century ago. It is still a challenging message and still raises up martyrs, such as the Guatemalan bishop Juan Gerardi, killed as recently as 1998[6], but there is far more unity and coherence within the Catholic community about this witness.

As many writers have pointed out, telling the story of martyrdom is an important act of 'memory' for the whole Christian community, but particularly for oppressed communities, as history is so often written by the 'victors', by the powerful.[7] There has been a wealth of writing and research about Romero since his death in 1980. The purpose of some of this has been to show that the archbishop was not martyred for political activism, or indeed simply for being 'on the side of the poor', but for his faithfulness to Christ and his Church, symbolised by his motto as a bishop: *sentir con la iglesia*, 'To feel with the Church'. We will see how his theology and teaching is deeply rooted in his love for the Church; there has also been much research done on how a strong ecclesiology, a strong doctrine of the Church is essential for the Church's witness in the face of persecution.[8] This research is helping the whole community as part of the beatification process, enabling us to form a rounded and balanced picture of Romero's ministry as a bishop, since much of what he taught and lived out in that ministry would have been important if he had not been martyred.

The life and teachings of Oscar Romero are a vast and evolving subject, and a booklet of this kind will necessarily leave out many details and perspectives. Fr James Brockman's biography[9] remains the most comprehensive account of the archbishop's life and death; the archbishop's own homilies and diary entries are an invaluable source of knowledge about his Christian witness and spirituality.

Early Life, Priest and Bishop

Life in El Salvador

It is impossible to understand Oscar Romero without knowing something about El Salvador. It is a small country perched on the edge of the pacific coast of central America, somewhat dwarfed by Honduras and Guatemala. Some facts and figures about the country give us a horrifying picture of injustice: 5 million population, 2% of people control 57% of usable land, 91% of people occupy only 21% of the land; 16 families own the same amount of land as is utilised by 230,000 rural families; 75% of children suffer serious malnutrition; 60% of children die at birth. 57% of population have safe drinking water and half the people cannot read or write.[10]

Early life

Oscar Arnulfo Romero y Goldamez was born on the feast of the Assumption of Our Lady, 15th August, in 1917, in the town of Ciudad Barrios in the mountains of El Salvador, near the border with Honduras. His mother was Guadalupe de Jesús Galdámez and his father Santos Romero, a telegrapher[11], and he was the second of seven children. The people of the town lived in great poverty - there was no electricity or running water in the house and the children slept on the floor, although the family were better off than many others; they had to rent rooms out in their house to make ends meet.[12] When Oscar was very young there was a visit to the town from the first bishop of San Miguel, Juan Antonio Duenas y Arguemedo - he accompanied the bishop on his visiting rounds and told him he wanted to be a priest; the bishop predicted that he would be a bishop. He was seen as a serious and reflective child, as his sister said: 'As a boy he seemed a little sad. My brother always turned inward, thought too much.'[13]

Oscar's family could not afford to continue his education beyond the age of twelve so he was apprenticed to a local carpenter. Although he showed promise in this craft he entered the minor seminary at San Miguel at the age of thirteen. He was bright and studious, progressing to the major seminary and eventually to the Gregorian University in Rome, where he gained his licentiate in theology.

Romero the priest

He was ordained priest in Rome in 1942, but as a result of the war his family were unable to travel to Rome for the event. He wanted to continue studies in Rome on ascetical theology, but as there was a severe shortage of priests in El Salvador he returned home in 1944, where he celebrated his 'first Mass' in his home village in January 1944.[14] He was appointed a parish priest in the cathedral parish of San Domingo in the city of San Miguel, where he stayed for over thirty years, but his administrative and intellectual gifts meant that this was combined with other posts: rector of the interdiocesan seminary, secretary of the diocese of San Miguel and chaplain of the Church of San Francisco.

During this time he was noted for his pastoral zeal, concern for the poor, and preaching; he was remembered by other priests as a man of fervent and disciplined prayer, renowned in the confessional. 'He gave shelter to drunken persons on the street and asked the wealthy for money, which he would redistribute to the hungry.'[15] He was a very hard worker and expected high standards of his colleagues in the priesthood, often unsuccessfully; others' shortcomings often simply increased his workload.[16] He was also seen as rather shy - he had difficulty in establishing dialogue with other priests and was sometimes impatient and some other priests saw him as a rather daunting workaholic. He was very critical of lax standards among other clergy - the failure to wear a cassock, womanising and excessive drinking. We see early signs at this stage of Romero's commitment to the poor in words we wrote in the journal *Chaparrastique*, of which he was director - but showing also a view of how the poor should 'help themselves' which would not later on be a feature of his commitment:

'This is the true Caritas, the one that is not only content to feed someone out of a noble enthusiasm to give aid in an emergency situation, but one which, looking toward a better future, also teaches the poor how to work in order to earn their livelihood and dignity.'[17]

Independent

He enjoyed good relationships as a priest with local wealthy landowners, factory magnates and coffee plantation owners; alms they gave to the Church were given to the poor. But an early sign of the resentment he could cause with the rich was when he upset local wealthy ladies in the parish who tried to refurbish and 'upgrade' his living accommodation when he was away on one occasion; on his return Romero got rid of all the new things they had put in and returned his room to its original austere state, making the comment, 'I may be their friend, but they're not going to start manipulating me, no matter how much money they have.'[18] One group whose enmity he did incur was the Freemasons - he refused to allow a hero of theirs to be commemorated in the cathedral, or the celebration of the funerals of masons.[19]

Medellín 1968

In 1967 he moved to San Salvador to become executive secretary of the Episcopal Council for Central America and Panama, secretary of the El Salvador Bishops'

Conference and editor of the archdiocesan newspaper, *Orientacion* - clearly he was a 'rising star'. Like others, he was profoundly affected by the Second CELAM Assembly at Medellín in Peru in 1968, one of the key events in the history of the Church in Latin America and in the development of the 'theologies of liberation'. It built on the teachings of Blessed John XXIII[20], Paul VI and Vatican II in developing the 'preferential option for the poor'. One of the documents says this:

'The Latin American Episcopacy cannot remain indifferent before the enormous social injustices existing in Latin America, injustices that maintain the majority of our people, in very many cases, on the verge of human misery. A silent clamour gushes from millions of people, asking their pastors for a liberation which does not come from anywhere. "You are now listening to us in silence, but we hear the cry which arises from their suffering," said the Pope to the peasants in Colombia.'[21]

For although many considered Romero at this point to have been theological conservative and alarmed by the direction the Church was taking after Vatican II, others claim that the picture was more complex. Archbishop Rodrigo Orlando Cabrera later wrote: 'When I returned from Medellín, I found him to be quite different. You could now speak to him about the social and political problems in the country.'[22]

Romero the bishop

As a rising star it was no surprise when he was appointed auxiliary Bishop of San Salvador in 1970, to assist Archbishop Luis Chávez. He was ordained bishop in the cathedral in the capital city, and it is worth noting that the priest friend he asked to organise the celebration was a Jesuit who taught at the seminary where Romero had been living, Fr Rutilio Grande. This priest had been a friend of Romero's since 1967, and he was at the forefront of those calling for spiritual and theological renewal after the Council - much more enthusiastically than Romero himself. By 1970 he was already a controversial figure, but he was also an accomplished liturgist with a good eye for detail.[23] Shortly after his episcopal ordination he went to Rome to thank Pope Paul VI for his naming, who gave him a chalice which he used for the rest of his life.

But Romero in this period was seen as uneasy about some post-Vatican II reforms. The day after he became a bishop the Bishops' Conference launched the 'First National Pastoral Week' in which priests like Fr Grande were heavily involved, wanting to implement the teachings of the Medellín assembly and of a recent meeting of Central American Bishops. The *Conclusions of the Pastoral Week* contained strong criticisms of injustices in the country and called for a strong commitment to the cause of the poor, but the Salvadoran Bishops Conference appointed a commission headed by Romero which drastically watered down its text. Fr Grande and the Jesuits enjoyed much support among clergy and the incident made public divisions within the Salvadoran church;[24] he was out of sympathy with the Jesuits responsible for running the seminary and helped to ensure their removal.[25] Other specific policies with which Romero seemed to be unhappy included giving responsibility to laypeople as catechists and 'Delegates of the Word', and he avoided clergy meetings. Someone said of him that he was 'strong willed and seemingly born to lead, yet he submitted unquestioningly to a structure that encourages conformity.'[26] He and the Bishops' Conference supported the military occupation of the university in July 1972.[27]

A new diocese

Consequently there was relief all round when he left the archdiocese in 1974 on his appointment as bishop of Santiago de María, his home diocese: it was a largely rural and mountainous diocese in the east of the country. Many parishes were only accessible by horse and mule and much of Romero's brief ministry as bishop was spent visiting them. He saw on these visits the sheer extent of grinding rural poverty:

'...children dying from curable diseases because their parents could not pay for immunisations or basic medications; people who were paid less than half of the legal minimum wage, if they were paid at all; people who had been savagely beaten for "insolence" when they asked for long overdue pay; children who had been systematically denied educational opportunity so they would have no alternatives to becoming field labourers; and victims of literally hundreds of other forms of mistreatment.'[28]

Poverty and growing violence

In a pastoral letter (November 1976) he reflected on the poverty of coffee plantation workers[29] and he made available diocesan and personal resources to help the poor. In terms of his theological and personal development, a key event was the massacre on 21st June 1975 of five *campesinos*, hacked to death by National Guardsmen in the tiny village of Tres Calles. Romero rushed to the village and celebrated the funeral Mass for the victims; he also publicly accused the military government of 'grim violations of human rights' and wrote a letter of protest to the head of the government, Colonel Armando Molina. He protested in person to the local National Guard commander, who ominously replied, pointing at him, 'Cassocks are not bullet-proof', the first of many death threats.[30] At this period Romero still seems to have thought of those in authority as being better than their subordinates, so he intervened on a 'high level' rather than publicly.

But the Bishop of Santiago de María was changing, evolving: another influence on him in this period was Paul VI's Post-Synodal Exhortation on Evangelisation, *Evangelii Nuntiandi*, published at the end of 1974. This ground-breaking document set the Church's message of liberation for the poor at the heart of its preaching of the gospel - it was not an afterthought or an 'optional extra'. The pope wrote about: 'the close links between evangelisation and human advancement, that is, development and liberation. There is a link in the anthropological order because the person to be evangelised is not an abstract being but someone subject to social and economic factors. There is also a connection in the theological sphere because the plan of creation cannot be isolated from the plan of redemption. There is, finally, a connection in the evangelical order, that is, the order of charity: for how can the new law be proclaimed unless it promotes a true practical advancement of man in a spirit of justice and peace.'[31]

The growing violence in the country and the terrible poverty he saw at first hand, alongside the ways in which Catholic teaching was developing, were helping him to see that charitable giving is not enough to help the poor - this has to be accompanied by campaigning for justice, by standing alongside the suffering in solidarity.

Archbishop of San Salvador

'Courage! You are the one in charge!'

Archbishop Chávez had been leader of El Salvador's metropolitan see since 1938. Because Romero was still seen by many as a conservative, out of tune with the thinking of Vatican II and the Medellín conference, many favoured to be his successor the man who had been his auxiliary bishop since 1960, Bishop Rivera (who was destined to succeed Romero). Consequently Romero's appointment in early 1977 dismayed many in the archdiocese and seems to have been welcomed by many in the oligarchy which controlled the country. Particularly in his early life, Romero had cultivated the friendship of the rich, so those who had been alarmed by Chávez' episcopate (including most of the other bishops) breathed a sigh of relief.

Both these reactions, of dismay and joy, were to be reversed very soon after Romero became archbishop. The ceremony at which he took canonical possession of the archdiocese on February happened in a period of great violence following fraudulently conducted elections. Shortly after the ceremony in the cathedral hundreds were killed in demonstrations in the centre of San Salvador. In the aftermath of the violence the Bishops' Conference issued a strong pastoral letter, read in all churches on 13th March. This powerfully condemned the violence and human rights abuses, showing a unity among the bishops which was not to recur very often after this. Romero hesitated about the letter being publicly read, and had to be encouraged to stand firm by his auxiliary Bishop Rivera.[32] A large number of demonstrators had recently been killed. The clouds of violence over the country were getting darker all the time.

First 100 days

From the beginning Romero surprised many by taking the trouble to listen to his priests and others. In his first message to the diocese he acknowledged humbly that some had not welcomed his appointment and the ministry of listening was to characterise his whole episcopate: his diary entries, which cover most of the second and third years of his ministry as archbishop are filled with long meetings with clergy, religious and laypeople with pastoral responsibilities, where people were given space to share their thoughts with their chief pastor: for example, his weekly homilies given at the 8am Mass in the cathedral, usually broadcast all over the country, were written after a meeting at which events of the last week were discussed so they could be alluded to in the homily. The context of violence and oppression during what

Romero's biographer calls the 'First Hundred days'[33] completed very quickly Romero's development, signs of which we have already seen, into a forthright defender of those whom the Old Testament calls the *anaw'im*, the 'poor of the land.'

Murder of Father Grande

In this time of violence and killing one event stands out: the murder of Romero's old friend, the Jesuit Fr Rutilio Grande, parish priest of Aguilares, who was shot in a field of sugar cane with an old man and a fifteen year boy who were accompanying him.[34] Romero reacted with great speed, going to the village. The funeral of Fr Grande and the two other victims took place in the cathedral, the Mass being celebrated by the Apostolic Visitor, Archbishop Emanuele Gerada.

He also took, after consultation with the priests of the archdiocese, a decision which would have far-reaching consequences for people's perceptions of him, and his relationships with his brother bishops: he decided that on the Sunday after the funeral, there would only be one Mass in the archdiocese, at the cathedral, which priests and laypeople from the whole Catholic community would be able to attend to mark the murder of Fr Grande. This caused consternation with many of the wealthy people in the diocese (who, ironically, were in a better position to get to a Mass in the centre of the city than the poor) and was also opposed by Archbishop Gerada,[35] and some of the other bishops. Catholic teaching about the unity of a diocese under the direction of its bishop is made vividly clear when the bishop celebrates a Mass for the whole diocese with his priests and people, as happens at the Chrism Mass on Maundy Thursday in every diocese and on other special occasions. To celebrate a single Sunday Mass for good pastoral reasons is well within a bishop's competence and was a strong sign of solidarity within the whole diocese, to strengthen people's faith. One of the priests who was present, the Jesuit theologian Fr Jon Sobrino, describes the tremendous pastoral effects of this single celebration - thousands made their confession before the Mass and received Holy Communion[36].

Visit to Pope Paul VI

The controversy with Archbishop Gerada, and his previous practice when he was made a bishop in 1970, now prompted Romero quickly to go to Rome and see Pope Paul VI and Vatican officials, at the end of the first month of his new ministry. He flew to Rome, prayed at the tomb of St Peter - and also at the tomb of Pius XI, who had been pope when he had begun his studies in Rome, and whose resistance to Fascism and Nazism Romero much admired - and had saw Cardinal Sebastian Baggio, the Prefect of the Congregation of the Bishops, and others. Romero was justifiably concerned at biased and hostile reports reaching Rome about his ministry, and this continued until his death. He also had a private audience with Paul VI and gave him a picture of Fr Grande. The Holy Father took both of Romero's hands in his and said to him: 'Courage! You are the one in charge.'[37]

'Be a patriot! Kill a priest!'

From the very time of the murders the archbishop attempted to get the State authorities to investigate properly what had happened so that the killers could be brought to justice, through strong letters to the President of the Republic. He was dissatisfied with the response and made it clear that he would not attend any State functions (including, at the beginning of July 1977, the inauguration of the new president) until the murders were properly investigated, and he stood by this decision for the remaining period of his life and ministry, a decision not emulated by other bishops. We can see in this approach the basis of his dealings with the State: he constantly called for dialogue and negotiation, but he was not going to enter a cosy or comfortable relationship with authorities whose conduct he was constantly questioning; but he combined this with personal courtesy and pastoral concern for individuals.[38]

Two months after the murder of Fr Grande the village of Aguilares was occupied for a month by the military. The archbishop attempted to go to the village but was prevented from getting in (even the military chaplain was arrested[39]); during the occupation the young bell-ringer and others were killed, the three priests in the parish were removed by the soldiers and expelled from the country. Other people were abducted and imprisoned, and the church was taken over by soldiers, who desecrated the Reserved Sacrament, shooting open the tabernacle and scattering hosts on the floor of the church. When the soldiers left Romero returned to the village on 19th June and celebrated a Mass with the people. At the beginning of his homily Romero said:

'It is my lot to gather up the trampled, the dead, and all that the persecution of the church leaves behind. I have come to recover a profaned church, tabernacle and people. Your sorrow is the Church's sorrow. You are the image of the divine one who was pierced.[40] It is the image of all the populations that, like Aguilares, are pierced through, and outraged. But if your suffering is done with faith and is given a redemptive meaning, then Aguilares is singing the precious stanzas of liberation. For when they look on him whom they have pierced, they will repent and will see the heroism and will see the joy of those whom the Lord blesses in their sorrow. Let there be no animosity in our heart. Let this Eucharist, which is a call to reconciliation with God and our brothers and sisters, leave in all our hearts the satisfaction that we are Christians…let us pray for the conversion of those who struck us…of those who sacrilegiously dared to lay hands on the sacred tabernacle. Let us pray to the Lord for forgiveness and for the due repentance of those who converted a town into a prison and a place of torment. Let the Lord touch their hearts…'[41]

At the end of the Mass the archbishop led a procession of the Host around the piazza outside the cathedral. There was tension at this point because of the presence near the Town Hall of soldiers and armed police, so that the procession hesitated for fear of people being shot; but Romero, carrying the monstrance, kept the procession moving with the word *Adelante*, 'let us go!'

Hatred against the Church

The desecration, shocking as it is (and it happened on other occasions[42]), shows us something profound. The violence of the security forces against the poor was linked closely to a deep hatred towards the Catholic Church, even though most of the perpetrators were baptised Catholics; the press attacks on Romero and many of his priests show the same violence. Dishonour done to the sacramental Body of Christ stands alongside the outrage done to the Body of Christ which is the Church by means of the torture and killing of men and women created in God's image. During the rest of this first year of his ministry as archbishop, Romero tried hard to get the State authorities to investigate properly who was responsible for the killings at Aguilares and elsewhere - a number of members of the *Cursillo* movement were killed in the autumn and at the end of the year another priest, Fr Molina. Romero was gaining much support, both from hundreds of poor people in El Salvador, and from leading churchmen and politicians abroad, including (at the beginning of 1978) Cardinal Basil Hume, Archbishop of Westminster, who sent money to help the pastoral work of the archdiocese and help repair the Catholic radio station, which was frequently bombed. Early in 1978 Romero was awarded an honorary degree by the Jesuit University of Georgetown in the United States, and at the end of the year nominated for the Nobel Peace Prize, an event which prompted an official visit to El Salvador by three British parliamentarians. Not long before his death, at the beginning of 1980, he was honoured with an honorary degree from the Catholic University of Louvain in Belgium.

Denouncing violence

The primary context for Romero's ministry as archbishop was the worsening violence in the country. His homilies - particularly those given at the 8am Mass in the cathedral which were normally broadcast around the country - made him a major national figure and the foremost critic of those carrying out the killings of so many people and the government which was unable or unwilling to control those responsible, let alone bring them to justice. He would consult many others before preaching and detail in his homilies violent events of the previous week: he did not stick to generalities, but rather listed in detail, based on accurate testimony, things that had been done. The violence which he denounced was directed against those involved in campaigning for a more just society, and in particular those linked to trade unions and specific popular movements - which the oligarchy and most people in the government saw as subversive and 'Marxist'.

Parish communities

Alongside these political groupings were the new ways in which parish communities were being organised in the light of the teachings of the Second Vatican Council, Paul VI and the CELAM assembly at Medellín in 1968: small groups led by trained lay catechists, meeting for study of the Bible, prayer and reflection. These groups often developed into what are known as 'Base Christian Communities', forming small cells or groups within the overall parish structure[43]. Catholics in these groups discussed how to apply the teachings of the Church about justice for the poor to the situation in the country, so they attracted the same anger and hatred as other organisations, and so did the priests and religious who guided them.

Those in Salvadoran society opposed to reform or democracy - the small number of families who owned most of the land and the wealth, many business leaders, the army and security forces - largely controlled the mass media (radio, television and newspapers) and Romero and many priests (particularly the Jesuits) were constantly subjected to abuse and attack. Posters appeared in San Salvador with these chilling words: 'Be a patriot! Kill a priest!' One headline in the tabloid paper *La Opinion* was 'MONS. ROMERO DIRIGE GRUPO TERRORISTA' (Romero is directing a terrorist group).[44]

At the beginning of 1979 there was a massacre the diocesan youth centre at Despertar, when the priest there, Fr Ortiz, and others were brutally killed[45] and later in the year Romero's friend Apolinario Serrano. The killings in country areas outside the city of San Salvador created a growing refugee problem, as many came to the city to seek safety, and Romero made accommodation available for the refugees at the seminary in the city and elsewhere[46] and from an early stage Romero set up a legal team to try and hold the security forces to account in the often ineffectual law courts of the country and give support to men and women who had been arrested.[47]

Clear sighted

However, it is not true to allege that Romero was simply allied with the 'popular' movements trying to bring about change. In his homilies and articles he frequently challenged the ways in which some of the groups worked[48], especially when they resorted to violence and kidnapping, and when people were taken hostage he frequently offered to act as intermediary to get hostages released. He also distanced the Church from uncritical adherence to Marxist ideology and called constantly for unity and reconciliation in Salvadoran society, not 'class war'. Other tactics also dismayed him, such as the occupation of foreign embassies and of churches, particularly his own cathedral, but he tried to engage in dialogue with the groups concerned rather than resort to condemnation or the use of violence; he was also clear on the particular responsibilities of clergy in relation to popular groups: as Catholic pastors they must not lose their independence.

Puebla

A major milestone in Romero's ministry as archbishop, and indeed in the history of the Church in Latin America, is the Third CELAM Assembly in Puebla (Mexico) in early 1979, postponed from 1978 because of the deaths of Paul VI and John Paul I. Just as Romero in his ministry as archbishop (like many others before him) had been inspired by the Second assembly in Medellín in 1978, so the assembly at Puebla - the nature of the gathering, John Paul II's opening address and the conference conclusions - was building-block in Romero's teaching during the last year of his life.

Romero was in Mexico for the assembly from 22nd January until 16th February:[49] he left straight after the funeral of Father Octavio Ortiz, killed as referred to above with four young men at a youth retreat centre in El Despertar while the town was being occupied by the military - the bodies of the shot men were disfigured by being run over by military vehicles. Part of the context for the assembly was the growth in the importance of theologies of liberation, particularly since the Medellín assembly in 1968, and also the intensifying rebellion against the Somoza dictatorship in Nicaragua. Romero's diary entries show how much he found the experience of the assembly rewarding and a source of spiritual strength for the remaining year of his ministry - not simply as a theological resource, but as a focussing of his prayer life.

The Church's disunity

In periods of history when the Church has been persecuted the ability of Christians to resist oppression has always been strengthened when the Church has been visibly united in its witness. In the early Church, when Christians apostasised and compromised with the Roman authorities, the canonical penalties were severe and penances had to be undergone before offenders could be absolved. In the 20th century, both in Eastern Europe under Communism (particularly in Poland) and in some parts of Latin America (by and large in Chile under Pinochet[50]) unity among the bishops of the Church was essential to the Church's resistance. Sadly such unity did not exist in El Salvador.

When Archbishop Chávez retired at the end of 1976 there were significant divisions among the bishops and had been for some time. The metropolitan and his auxiliary Bishop Rivera had embraced the renewal of the Church after Vatican II and the insights of Medellín, and encouraged pastoral policies which reflected this direction.

Those who had opposed Chávez hoped for a change of policy under Romero, known to be cautious and broadly conservative; for this reason they felt particularly angry that Romero, almost from the very beginning of his ministry as archbishop, continued and furthered his predecessor's policies - and indeed, because of his skills as a broadcaster and speaker, became very rapidly a much better known spokesman for the Church and an opponent of the rich and the powerful. As we saw above, in the very early days after Romero became archbishop there was a united and forthright response to the constant killings and the murder of Fr Rutilio Grande, but this unity did not last. From Romero's diaries and the records of the Bishops' Conference the heart of the problem was that four of the six bishops, while not condoning the killing of priests, thought that they and their communities had brought violence upon themselves by being led by Marxist revolutionaries; and that the Church should not antagonise the government and security services - Romero and Rivera were seen as pawns of these radical priests, particularly the Jesuits. Their foremost critics were Bishop Aparicio, President of the Bishops' Conference, and Bishop Alvarez who was both a diocesan bishop and Military Vicar (that is, in modern parlance, Bishop of the Forces) - he held the rank of colonel in the armed forces. Romero's critics were backed by the nuncio, Archbishop Gerada. While the divisions were constant for most of the time Romero was archbishop, it was focussed on certain specific issues such as Romero's decision to hold a single Mass in the archdiocese after Fr Grande's death, a letter from priests all over the country to the papal nuncio criticising his policies, the running of the national seminary in San Salvador and the use of the seminary buildings by the archdiocese. This would not have been too bad if the divisions had remained private within a small number of bishops, but sadly they became public - over differing decisions about attending state functions, and pointed criticisms made of Romero by Bishop Aparicio at a press conference during the Puebla assembly. Many of these tensions did not disappear after Romero's death. Romero's diary entries and letters show how distressed he was by this disunity - much of the criticism was personal, which pained him as he had known the bishops concerned for many years.[51] Some of this did not finish when Romero was killed: some of the bishops were not at the funeral Mass and three years later, during Pope John Paul's visit, one of them attacked Romero's memory.

Romero and Rome

This scandalous disunity caused great concern to the Holy See - indeed, this predates Romero's ministry as archbishop; it was necessary for the archbishop, all the time, to 'watch his back' and ensure that the Holy See had a full and accurate picture of his ministry, in the face of so many slurs from his colleagues and from the pope's official representative in the country. Romero had trained for the priesthood in Rome and had a deep devotion to the Vicar of Christ, so it pained him that an inaccurate and misleading picture of his ministry was being relayed to the Vatican. It is a tribute to his skill that he managed to circumvent these lines of communication and retain the personal confidence of two popes.

We have already seen how Romero went quickly to Rome to see Paul VI and Cardinal Baggio at the end of his first month as archbishop in May 1977. This was prompted by the seriousness of the situation in the country, but also by awareness that early decisions he had taken had been controversial among his colleagues, particularly the single Sunday Mass after the killing and funeral of Fr Rutilio Grande. By May 1978 divisions within the bishops' conference and many other problems led to concerned dialogue between Romero and the Congregation of Bishops in Rome, and he was invited to Rome - the bishops were due to make their five-yearly *ad limina* visit to the Holy See, but their divisions made this impossible.[52] Before he went Romero sent Baggio a twenty-three page letter reviewing his ministry and responding to criticisms which he knew had been made about him to Rome from some of his brother bishops. His interview with Baggio in Rome was difficult, but during it and subsequently he responded to the criticisms which had been made.[53] The highlight of his visit was a private audience with the Holy Father himself. The pope grasped his hand for a long time and said, 'I understand your difficult work, It is a work that can be misunderstood; it requires a great deal of patience and a great deal of strength. I already know that not everyone thinks like you do, that it is difficult in the circumstances of your country to have this unanimity of thinking. Nevertheless, proceed with courage, with patience, with strength, with hope.'[54] They had a very warm conversation and were photographed together; Romero left a private memorandum with the pope expressing regret at the negative view being created of him in Rome, but reiterating his loyalty to the successor of Peter.

Negative reports persist

Romero's third visit to Rome as archbishop was a year later, after the deaths of Paul VI, John Paul I and the delayed Puebla assembly. This took place a few months after a visitation to the archdiocese by a special *Apostolic Visitor*, Bishop Antonio Quarracino and at about the same time as an attack on him written to the Holy See by four of the other bishops.[55] He went partly for a beatification ceremony[56] but also to meet the new pope, John Paul II. He had learnt by this time that Bishop Quarracino had suggested that divisions in the church could be healed by the appointment of an 'Apostolic Administrator' who would take over many of Romero's duties, so much of the visit was taken up with trying to stop this proposal from taking effect. Again, the meeting with the pope was very cordial, discussing the need for prudence and the dangers of the bishops being so disunited. Romero wrote, 'I left, pleased by the meeting, but worried to see how much the negative reports of my pastoral work had influenced him, although deep down I remembered that he had recommended "courage and boldness, but, at the same time, tempered with the necessary prudence and balance."'[57] Fortunately the idea of an administrator came to nothing.

Love and obedience

He met John Paul again in January 1980, when he was able to visit Rome while in Europe to receive an honorary degree from the Catholic University of Louvain in Belgium. On this occasion he saw Romero privately after a General Audience, and 'he received me very warmly and told me that he understood perfectly how difficult the political situation of my country is…the pope said that he agreed with everything that I was saying and, at the end, he gave me a very fraternal embrace and told me that he prayed every day for El Salvador.'[58]

Romero's meetings with two popes during the time of his ministry as archbishop are important because they show us so many things: his deep and filial love for the Church and for Peter's successors; how damaging the campaign against him by his colleagues was; but how effectively he rebutted the charges against him, so that by the time of his martyrdom his position as archbishop and metropolitan had never been stronger. The claim sometimes made by his opponents that he was at odds with the teachings of Paul VI and John Paul II is entirely false: if that had been the case, the Holy See would hardly have appointed as his successor the one bishop in El Salvador who was allied to his policies, Bishop Rivera.

Teaching of Oscar Romero

When he became a bishop in 1970 Oscar Romero chose as his motto *Sentir con la iglesia*, 'To be of one mind with the Church'. We cannot adequately understand the depth of his ministry as archbishop unless we realise how deeply imbued he was with a love of the Church, the people of God. As has been shown in other but similar contexts, Christians resist most effectively the violence of tyrannical regimes when they have a strong or 'high' doctrine of the Church as the visible and 'real' Body of Christ on earth - so when priests and laypeople are tortured or killed, the whole body suffers with them.[59] It is clear from Romero's teaching ministry in his time as archbishop that if he had not suffered martyrdom he would still be considered a major teacher of the Catholic faith in the 20th century. The sadness is, as we reflected above, that he was undermined by other Catholics and teachers of the faith.

Impressive output

In many ways his 'output' was prolific. For most of his time as archbishop his Sunday homilies were delivered at the 8am Mass in his cathedral or at another large church in the centre of San Salvador.[60] These were usually broadcast

live by the archdiocesan radio station, YSAX, and became a centre of opposition to repression and violence, particular as most of the written media was controlled by those opposed to social change. In many ways this prominence was what made Romero so important - he was able to cut through the control of the media by the rich and powerful and give a voice to the poor and oppressed. Although the radio station could be bombed, it was hard for it to be officially silenced. As his ministry developed Romero used his Sunday homilies very intelligently: he always referred to specific events which had happened in the last week, and he also took advice from others in consultative meetings about what the themes of the homily should be. At the same time it is clear from the texts that what the archbishop taught was always firmly rooted in the scripture readings set for each particular Sunday or other occasion. The preaching of the word of God is always to be so based on the lectionary, and Romero's abilities as a preacher show him to be master of his craft; his skills had been built up over the whole of his ministry as a priest and a bishop, and he began to be renowned as a preacher and broadcaster in the 1950s.

Teaching in pastoral letters

Our clearest picture of his developed teaching comes from the four pastoral letters he wrote as Archbishop of San Salvador. He wrote an initial letter as well to the

priests of the archdiocese issued in February 1977 at the
time of his appointment; his first pastoral letter was
written for Easter 1977; the remaining three came out
each year at the time of the national religious festival for
a country dedicated to the Saviour, the feast of the
Transfiguration, 6th August. While seeing Romero as an
outstanding teacher of the faith, we should also be clear
that he was part of an enormous and flowering tradition,
made explicit in the teachings of the Latin American
bishops at Medellín and Puebla.

Romero's initial letter to his priests was not intended to
be a significant teaching document, but rather an
introduction of Romero as pastor, conscious that many
were unhappy at his appointment. The letter was an offer
of friendship: 'I wish to tell you of the spirit of cooperation
that I offer you and that I need from you so that together
we can share the honour that Christ gives us of helping him
build the church, each one in his own vocation'[61]

He went on to remind his priests that they needed to
form a friendship 'based on our faith in the sacramental
reality that identifies us with the one priesthood of Christ
and that bears the human warmth of understanding, of
mutual respect and forgiveness, of honesty, loyalty and
all the human virtues that nourish our supernatural
communion on the natural and psychological levels.' He
went on to invite the priests to the ceremony when he was
due to take canonical possession of the archdiocese and to

dinner, and also made it clear that they were always welcome to stay in the seminary.

The funerals of murdered priests were sad landmarks in Romero's ministry as archbishop. We can only fully understand how important these events were to him by considering two things: first, his sense of outrage that these devoted pastors were brutally killed for their faithfulness to the gospel, for their love for and solidarity with the poor; and second, the close theological and canonical bonds between priests and their bishop. This relationship is a key Catholic teaching, creating a personal relationship of love and interdependence, in many ways distinctive to the Catholic Church. A bishop does not often have to bury so many of his devoted priests in these circumstances, most of them younger than him, and this shows us what this relationship means at its most profound.

The Paschal Church

The Easter pastoral is the first glimpse we have of Romero's sustained and reflective teaching ministry, entitled *The Paschal Church*. He described the archdiocese as living a 'paschal hour' made real in the liturgy, and he wanted everyone to be involved in a 'reflective dialogue' with the church 'which is always desirous of dialogue with all in order to communicate to them the truth and the grace that God has entrusted it for guiding the world according his divine plans…the church does not live for itself, but to bring to the world the truth and the grace of the paschal mystery.' He went on to reflect on the Exodus experience in the paschal mystery - the people of Israel passage 'from slavery through sea and desert to a promised land, to freedom and repose.' Jesus' own death and resurrection transform these symbols and preparations in reality - his death destroys the reign of sin, and his resurrection 'implants now in history the reign of eternal life and offers us the capacity for the most daring transformation of history and of life.' This leads Romero into a deep reflection about the nature of the Church:

'The Church is the body of the risen Christ, and by baptism all the members that make it up live that tension of Passover, that passage from death to life, that passage that never ends called conversion, which is the unceasing demand to kill in oneself all that is sin and make live with ever growing power all that is life, renewal, holiness and justice.' The Church is a community which is the sign of new life, and its preaching is the truth that saves; he cites the bishops at the Medellín conference who 'realised that the Spirit of the Passover urgently impelled our Church to dialogue and service towards our peoples.'

Medellín had stated that the Church could not be indifferent to the 'silent cry from millions of people begging their pastors for a liberation they find nowhere else.' He also draws on the teaching of Paul VI in *Evangelii Nuntiandi* and the whole letter sets a powerful blueprint for his ministry as archbishop[62].

The Body of Christ in history

This strong theology of the Church as the Body of Christ is developed more in the second pastoral letter, written a few months later in August 1977. It became Romero's custom to issue a letter to mark the 'feast of title' of the archdiocese and the nation of El Salvador, the feast of the Transfiguration of Christ on 6th August, and the remaining three letters mark this feast. The 1977 letter is about the ways in which the Church's self-understanding has developed in our own time:

'This is the theme of my letter: the Church is the body of Christ in history. By this I mean that Christ has wanted the Church to live in every period in history. The Church's founding is not to be understood in a legal, juridical manner, as though Christ had got a few men together to entrust them with a teaching and given them a charter, while remaining himself separate from the organisation. Rather, the origin of the Church is something much deeper. Christ founded his Church in order to keep on being present himself in the history of human beings, precisely through that group of Christians who form the Church. The Church is thus the flesh in which Christ incarnates throughout the ages his own life and the mission of his person.'

This means that the Church needs to change and adapt if it is be faithful: 'In the different circumstances of history, the criterion that guides the Church is not the satisfaction of human beings or its fear of them, no matter how powerful or feared they may be, but its duty to lend to Christ through history its voice so that Jesus can speak, its feet so that he can walk the world of today, its hands to work in the building up of the kingdom in today's world, and all its members to "fill up what is lacking in his suffering" (*Col* 1:24)'

So he refutes the accusations that the Church is preaching hatred and violence, that it had become Marxist, and that it had gone beyond the bounds of its mission. Rather, the Church's faithfulness was now leading to persecution and martyrdom, and also to a greater sense of solidarity and unity.[63] The vision he articulates is so rich in its picture of the Church; as Margaret Swedish, Director of the Religious Task Force in Central America, writes: 'It is precisely here that the prophetic witness of Oscar Romero is fully integrated with the institutional Church he led, for he put the Church at the service of this saving action of God, of Jesus Christ still present and active in history.'[64]

The Church and the peasant unions

Romero's third pastoral in 1978, a year later, was also signed by Bishop Rivera, now Bishop of Santiago de María - the occasion of the letter, the feast of the Transfiguration, was the day Pope Paul VI died. The letter addressed two subjects - the relationship between the Church and the peasant unions, FECCAS and UTC, and the use of violence. The first subject was covered in a detailed study of the place of trade unions in the social doctrine of the Catholic Church since the time of Leo XIII's 1891 encyclical *Rerum Novarum*[65] and other teachings of the Magisterium[66]: Romero and Rivera contrast the restrictions placed on the peasant union with the freedom given to the government-backed bodies, and they detail the nature of right involvement in the organisations, especially on the part of priests and religious. In a word, the Church supports the unions, but is also called to enlighten their efforts for human liberation with Christian teaching. For the Christian, integral human liberation 'embraces the whole human being in every dimension, including openness to the absolute that is God...it proceeds from a gospel vision of human nature and is based on deep motives of justice in charity. It has within it a truly spiritual dimension and has as its final goal salvation and happiness in God. It demands conversion of heart and mind and is not satisfied with merely changing structures. It excludes violence, which it considers "unchristian and unevangelical"[67], ineffective and not consonant with people's dignity.' The letter accepts that Christians, including those with pastoral responsibilities, will support the work of the unions, but urges them to put their faith first and preserve their independence - the role of priests needs to be worked out in consultation with the bishop. 'Base Christian communities' in many parishes were linked to the organisations.

The other question examined in the letter was very delicate. The popular organisations and unions had been the object of sustained violence from the security forces of the State (the police and the army) and from right-wing militias and 'death squads' for many years - how far were people allowed to defend themselves? The letter looks in depth at the whole of the Christian tradition in moral theology of 'just insurrection'; it reasserts what Paul VI said that in certain exceptional cases insurrection might be justified[68] and points out that the roots of violence in El Salvador lie in injustice - 'We fraternally invite all, especially the organisations that labour in the struggle for justice, to continue courageously and honestly with just objectives and to use legitimate means of pressure and not put all their trust in violence.'[69]

Although the letter was dated 6th August it did not actually appear until three weeks later; Romero added a tribute to the memory of Paul VI. Unexpectedly a statement appeared shortly after from the remaining four bishops which adopted a very different tone, virtually condemning the unions as Marxist; thus divisions in the hierarchy were made very public.

The mission of the Church in the nation's crisis

The purpose of Romero's last pastoral letter, in August 1979, was to 'present officially to the archdiocese the total spirit of Puebla' and its thought is dominated by the assembly a few months before; like other letters it is also the fruit of consultation and information drawn from the clergy of the archdiocese. The archbishop applied Puebla's teachings to his own country, detailing examples of social injustice and the unfair treatment of the organisations of the poor and the oppressed - and what he says is backed up by detailed statistics which had been gathered about killings and arrests. He accused the government directly of armed right-wing militias.

He analysed sin made real in the ways employers deprived workers of their rights, but also in unjust strikes and dishonesty among workers; sin also in bribery other forms of corruption, sexual exploitation, prostitution and drug abuse; sin made real as well in kidnappings and threats. Sins in society are forms of idolatry, ways in which the State seeks and usurps absolute power.[70] Nor does he shy away from the divisions within the Church, but recognises these and acknowledges his own responsibility.

Puebla had enunciated the key concept of the 'preferential option for the poor' and Romero says that this 'which the gospel demands of Christians, does not polarise or divide, but is rather a force for unity, because "it does not try to exclude other representatives of the social picture in which we live...but is an invitation to all, regardless of class, to accept and take up the cause of the poor as though accepting and taking up their own cause, the cause of Christ himself."'[71]

The letter also considers some of the issues which had arisen before, such as the use of violence and Marxism, and reiterates things had been said in earlier letters - the treatment of Marxism reflects faithfully the position of Puebla: using critically some Marxist tools is different from signing up to Marxist ideology, and 'the fear of Marxism keeps many from confronting the oppressive reality of liberal capitalism. Before the danger of a system clearly marked by sin, they forget to denounce and combat the reality imparted by another system equally marked by sin...the best way to overcome Marxism is to take seriously the preferential option for the poor.'

The letter also lays down conditions for constructive dialogue with the government and looks at developing pastoral policies for the archdiocese (which went back long before he became archbishop). The letter is a very thorough summary of his teaching; at the time of his death in 1980 Romero was beginning to prepare another pastoral on catechesis.[72]

The *corpus* of Romero's teaching shows him to be a consummate and mature teacher of the Catholic faith. He draws on the fullness of Catholic tradition and roots his teaching in his own prayer and in the liturgical life of the Church; he also applies Christian insights again and again to the violence and suffering of his people, but with humility and grace. What is also remarkable is the extent to which he collaborated with others in the writing of these major documents, often with detailed and specific references, so that they are not simply a testimony to his teaching but the whole life of the Church in the Archdiocese of San Salvador. Alongside his Sunday homilies they portray the authentic Christian shepherd at the heart of the life of his damaged people.

Sanctity of Oscar Romero

The word *romero* in Spanish means 'pilgrim'; we can see in Oscar Romero's life a progression in holiness, a pilgrimage, just as the Second Vatican Council sees the Church as the pilgrim people of God. This notion ought to help us to understand shifts in Romero's thinking. An accusation made against him in 1979 was that he had claimed to have undergone a 'conversion' when he became archbishop which led him to repudiate his past ministry and what he had learnt before. This slur misses the point not only about Romero but about Christian life in general - all of us are called to undergo a constant process of conversion, of looking at our lives, and seeking again and again God's forgiveness as we turn back to him. What we can see in his life and writings are clear signs of what the Church calls 'heroic sanctity' - an openness to God's will, a constant awareness of God's presence in his life.

Open and self-effacing

A Shepherd's Diary gives a very clear picture of humility, a daunting tendency to be self-effacing. In the face of great pressures in his ministry as archbishop, far greater than what he had encountered in his earlier life as a priest and a bishop, there is in its pages an overwhelming sense of calm, but also of a man conscious that he was in some ways feeling his way. The accusation made by some of his opponents that he was easily influenced by others again misses the point. Respect for others, a wish to engage in dialogue, above all a determination to listen to people - these are signs of strength in pastoral ministry and leadership, not weakness. We know too from other sources that he was no 'plaster saint' - at a retreat he made with other priests towards the end of his life it is recorded that his colleagues were open with him about his faults, such as his tendency to be irritable.[73]

Asking forgiveness

Willingness to admit mistakes is a good sign of holiness. In 1972 with the other bishops he had been responsible for removing the Jesuits from control of the national seminary; as archbishop he apologised for this.[74] As Fr Campbell-Johnson points out,[75] another example is the two visits he made to the parish of Zacamil on the outskirts of San Salvador. He went first when he was auxiliary bishop in 1972 - a dispute broke out between Romero and the Parish Priest over the Bishops' Conference support for the sacking of the national university by the army: the Mass had to be discontinued. Romero returned to the parish six years later and said at the beginning of Mass: 'You remember, we couldn't celebrate the Eucharist that day for the row there was between us. I remember it well and today, as your pastor, I want to tell you I now understand what happened and that I publicly admit before all of you my error. I was mistaken: you were right and you gave me that day a lesson in the faith, a lesson in what the Church is. Please forgive me for what took place.' It is also wrong to give the impression that he was only in one narrow spiritual tradition. Like many of his generation he was steeped in Ignatian spirituality and made the exercises in his early ministry; but this did not stop him having sharp differences with priests of the Society of Jesus at various times in his ministry. He also had strong links with the lay *Cursillo* movement (many of whose members were murdered in the course of their work) and right up to the last day of his life he maintained good relationships with members of *Opus Dei*, and for many years had a confessor from the prelature.

Spirituality

In Latin America local celebrations in churches and villages are often very important to people, as in other places, and this requires of a bishop an ability to attune himself to the spirituality of each community. For example, when Romero preached at the church of Our Lady of Mount Carmel in July 1977 he talked of the giving of the scapular to the English Carmelite St Simon Stock, as a sign of persecution in time of suffering: 'The Blessed Virgin offers us a promise of salvation. But it is not just a salvation after death. It is a salvation also here in history. And it demands inner renewal, the kingdom of God hat begins here on earth, within our own hearts... The promise that the Blessed Virgin wants to awaken in the human heart is an eschatological sense, a hope of the beyond - to work on this earth with the heart and soul in heaven, to know that no one takes up residence in this world but is, rather, on a pilgrimage to eternity, that the things of the earth pass away, that the eternal is what remains. Above all, it is this: transcendence... When Christ speaks of salvation, it must be considered in the way that the Church of 1977, assisted by the Holy Spirit, understands what salvation is... Society is what must be saved, the whole world...not the soul at the hour of death, but the person living in history must be saved' If the Blessed Virgin were to give the scapular to Simon Stock today, she would tell him: 'This is the sign of protection, a sign of God's teaching, a sign of humanity's integral vocation, for the salvation of the whole person, now, in this life. All who wear the scapular must be persons now who live now in salvation on this earth, must feel content to develop their human powers for the good of others.'

Simplicity: the Cross

Romero's basic spirituality was deep but simple. He used to like to pray the rosary while being driven on car journeys (which were very long to many places in his diocese); when he became archbishop he shunned offers of grand housing and lived initially in a room near the chapel of a hospital for cancer sufferers, and then in a small bungalow built for him in the hospital grounds. He had a deep and abiding love of Jesus in the Blessed Sacrament, shown in his horror at the acts of desecration committed in his churches.[76]

Oscar Romero's sanctity can be traced throughout his life. These are verses he wrote about his priesthood when he was a teenager:

'Your word is pardon and gentleness for the penitent,
Your word is holy instruction, eternal teaching;
It is light to brighten, advice to hearten;
It is voice of hope, fire that burns,
Way, truth, sublime splendour,
Life…eternity…
But no is the temple alone your battlefield;
You range the world with your sword upraised,
The redeeming cross.'[77]

In his early priesthood he had a strong *spirituality of the Cross*.[78] The trials he bore as archbishop in the last years of his life, and his martyrdom, can be seen to be rooted in this understanding.

Inner life

As was true of many Catholics of his age, things he wrote about his spiritual life are dominated by what is often termed now as 'scrupulosity' - a perhaps excessive urge to look at every detail of one's life for even the smallest signs of sin. The distance and reserve people detected in his early priesthood and episcopate can perhaps be linked to this, but even at the end of his life Romero looked closely at every aspect of his life and identified ways in which he failed to live a good Christian life. At the same time, the picture we have in his last years of how he relaxed - with the families of lay friends, enjoying the company of children, watching television, going to the circus - show us a man in maturity who is at ease with himself.

A Christian's spiritual life has to be about love. This was the verdict of the Jesuit theologian Jon Sobrino ten years after Romero's death:

'Archbishop Romero genuinely loved his people. He *only* loved them. He did not do as others, who, while loving the people, seek also their own personal, partisan, church interests. Archbishop Romero's love for his people caused him to relativise all else beside. As a result he could risk all that was not love for his people, even the institutional element in the church, even his own life.'[79]

What he said at his last retreat is perhaps the best picture we have of his sanctity:

'My other fear is for my life. It is not easy to accept a violent death, which is very possible in these circumstances, and the apostolic nuncio to Costa Rica warned me of imminent danger just this week. You have encouraged me, reminding me that my attitude should be to hand my life over to God regardless of the end to which that life might come: that unknown circumstances can be faced with God's grace; that God assisted the martyrs, and that if it comes to this I shall feel God very close as I draw my last breath; but that more valiant than surrender in death is the surrender of one's whole life - a life lived for God.'[80] Romero's confessor, Fr Secundo Azcue, subsequently said, 'I dare to consider this last retreat of his as his prayer in the garden. Archbishop Romero foresaw his very probable and imminent death. He felt terror at it as Jesus did in the garden. But he did not leave his post and his duty, ready to drink the chalice that the Father might give him to drink'[81]

Martyrdom of Oscar Romero

Archbishop Oscar Romero's ministry as head of the diocese of San Salvador had been characterised by a defence of the rights and dignity of the poor, the overwhelming majority of the people of his country. This defence had been marked by his reaction to the deaths of so many people at the hands of the security forces and shadowy death squads - most dramatically, the killing of many priests of the Archdiocese of San Salvador, bound in a unique theological way with their bishop (in practice, this closeness also existed with priests of religious orders, although their canonical relationship with him was different). So often a failure to understand why he was so affected by the deaths of his priests shows ignorance of this tenet of Catholic teaching; indeed, in other parts of the Catholic world there is a reduced sense of personal loyalty to the bishops of the Church.[82]

Political independence

By the end of 1979 Romero was strong and assertive in his ministry. The attitude of other bishops should not blind us to the fact that countless Catholics in El Salvador were inspired by his teachings and ministry, the poor, the oppressed, the downtrodden; his opponents in Salvadoran society, and in the Church, were alarmed by this, trying to minimise the importance of these events. In the autumn of 1979 the ineptitude of the government of President Carlos Romero (no relation) finally led to a coup by middle-ranking army officers (of which Archbishop Romero had some knowledge); in the early months after the coup he and others in the Church had hopes that there would be a marked improvement in the running of the country, and some Christian Democrat politicians who were close to the archbishop took up posts in the government. Indeed, if proof were needed of his political independence we can see this in the negative reaction from some on the political Left to his cautiously positive attitude to the new *junta*.

Death threats

By the beginning of 1980, however, enlightened elements in the government had been sidelined and the country drifted more and more into violence. In February Romero went to Europe to be honoured at Louvain University (and, as we saw above, saw the pope) but the situation at home become worse and worse. Romero was not unused to death threats, but at this time the papal nuncio to nearby Costa Rica passed on specific intelligence of threats to his life, and the foreign minister of Nicaragua offered him a place of refuge if he wished to leave El Salvador (a step he ruled out). In the Christian year Lent is a time for conversion and renewal, a period of spiritual intensity. As

Romero began this season in which he was to die, we can see so many signs of this, on different levels.

Letter to President Carter

One of the most remarkable things he did in the last month or so of his life was to write a letter to the US President Jimmy Carter. This was because it was reported that the USA was planning send substantial military aid to the government of El Salvador - at the end of 1979 it had already sent gas masks and bullet-proof vests. 'Your government's contribution', he wrote, 'instead of favouring greater justice and peace in El Salvador, will undoubtedly sharpen the injustice and the repression suffered by the organised people, whose struggle has often been for respect for their most basic human rights... You say that you are Christian. If you are really Christian, please stop sending military aid to the military here, because they use it only to kill my people.'

The archbishop read the letter out in the homily on the Sunday before Lent, before he sent it; it caused consternation at home and abroad; some commentators think that this intervention finally caused the death squads to resolve to have Romero killed. Reflecting on the Beatitudes, he also said, 'Blessed are you poor, for yours is the kingdom of God. You are the ones most able to understand what is not understood by those who are on their knees before false idols and who trust in them. You that do not have these idols, you that do not trust in them because you have no money or power, you that are destitute of everything: the poorer you are, the more you possess God's kingdom, provided you truly live that spirituality. The poverty that Jesus Christ here sanctifies is not simply a material poverty, not just having nothing - that is bad. It is a poverty that awakens consciousness, a poverty that accepts the cross and sacrifice, but not out of mere compliance, because it knows that such is not God's will.'[83]

Tensions rising

Tensions were getting worse: the day after this homily the Church's radio transmitter was destroyed by a bomb. The incident shocked many all over the world, and money was raised for its replacement: people on subsequent Sundays that Lent brought tape recorders to the archbishop's Mass so that the homilies could be shared later in groups. On the first Sunday of Lent, he was preaching about Christ's temptation in the wilderness, denouncing the idolatry of power and wealth. He issued this call to the rich of his country:

'If they won't listen to me, let them at least listen to the voice of Pope John Paul II, who this very week, at the beginning of Lent, exhorted the Catholics of the world to give up superfluous wealth in order to help the needy as a sign of Lenten penance... The pope said that the Church's concern is not only that there be a fairer sharing of wealth,

but that this sharing be because people have an attitude of
wanting to share not only possessions but life itself with
those who are disadvantaged in our society. This is
beautiful. Social justice is not just a law that mandates
sharing. Seen in a Christian manner, it is an internal
attitude like that of Christ, who, being rich, became poor
so as to be able to share his love with the poor. I hope that
this call of the Church will not further harden the hearts of
the oligarchs but will move them to conversion. Let them
share what they are and have. Let them not keep on
silencing with violence the voice of those of us who offer
this invitation. Let them not keep on killing those of us
who are trying to achieve a more just sharing of the power
and wealth of our country. I speak in the first person,
because this week I received notice that I am to be
eliminated next week. But let it be known that no one can
any longer kill the voice of justice.'[84]

Also in these weeks of Lent Romero publicly
associated himself with plans which were being drawn up
for the running of the country if things were to improve;
as he had the previous October he gave support to people
of good will - it was 'a further step in the process of
unification.' The cathedral in San Salvador was occupied
by protest groups who were unable to challenge the
government in any other way[85], so his Sunday homilies
were delivered at Mass in the nearby Sacred Heart

basilica. He reflected on specific government plans (such as land reform and the nationalisation of the banks) and also on the gradual disintegration of the new *junta* as Christian Democrat politicians felt increasingly unable to work with the military. As March 1980 continued more centres in the capital city were opened for refugees from outlying districts, victims of oppression from the security forces, and acts of violence were committed by them against the parish of Zacamil, and in the aftermath of this Romero preached one of his longest homilies (an hour and three-quarters) on the parable of the Prodigal Son - he included specific appeals to different groups within Salvadoran society. More deaths followed.

His final homily

His final Sunday homily on 23rd March gives us one of the clearest examples of his teaching, his courage and his ability to deliver teaching in a direct and challenging way. The radio station had been repaired. He said:

'I have been trying during these Sundays of Lent to uncover in divine revelation, in the word read here at Mass, God's programme to save peoples and individuals. Today, where history offers our people various proposals, we can say with assurance: the programme that better reflects God's programme will prevail. And this is the Church's mission, And so, in the light of God's word revealing God's plan for the happiness of peoples, we have the duty of also pointing out the realities, of seeing how God's plan is reflected among us or despised among us. Let no one take it ill that in the light of God's words read in our Mass we illuminate social, political and economic realities. If we did not, this would not be our own Christianity. It is thus that Christ willed to become incarnate, so that the light that he brings from the Father may become the life of people and of nations. I know that many are scandalised at what I say and charge that it forsakes the preaching of the gospel to meddle in politics. I do not accept that accusation. No, I strive that we may not just have on paper and study in theory all that Vatican Council II and the meetings at Medellín and Puebla have tried to further in us, but that we may live it and interpret it in this conflict-ridden reality, preaching the gospel as it should be preached for our people. I ask the Lord during the week, while I gather the people's cries and the sorrow stemming from so much crime, the ignominy of so much violence, to give me the fitting word to console, to denounce, to call to repentance. And though I continue to be a voice that cries in the desert, I know that the Church is making the effort to fulfil its mission.'

Detailing the violence of the previous week Romero preached about liberation.[86] What was remembered most about this last full-scale homily was the archbishop's appeal to those in power and to the men of violence:

'I would like to appeal in a special way to the army's enlisted men, and in particular to the ranks of the Guardía Nacional and the police - those in the barracks. Brothers: you are part of our own people. You kill your own campesino brothers and sisters. And before an order to kill that a man may give, God's law must prevail that says: Thou shalt not kill! No soldier is obliged to obey an order against the law of God. No one has to fulfil an immoral law. It is time to take back your consciences and to obey your consciences rather than the orders of sin. The Church, defender of the rights of God, of the law of God, of human dignity, of the person, cannot remain silent before such abomination. We want the government to understand seriously that reforms are worth nothing if they are stained with so much blood. In the name of God, and in the name of this suffering people, whose laments rise to heaven each day more tumultuous, I beg you, I beseech you, I order you in the name of God: Stop the repression!…the Church preaches its liberation just as we have studied it today in the Holy Bible - a liberation that includes, above all, respect for the dignity of the person, the salvation of the people's common good, and transcendence, which looks before all to God, and from God alone derives its hope and its force.'[87]

For Romero's opponents this was simply a call to military insurrection: nothing captures so well the clarity of his message against violence and false loyalties.

His last day

The following day, Monday 24th March, seemed a quiet day for the archbishop, involving lunch with some priests from *Opus Dei*, a doctor's appointment for an ear infection and a visit to his confessor. In the evening he was due to say a Mass in the chapel of the hospital where he lived for the soul of the mother of a friend of his, Jorge Pinto[88], who had died a year before. It was a simple Mass attended by Doña Sarita Pinto's family and friends, together with sisters, nurses and patients of the hospital. The liturgy of this Memorial Mass helps our understanding.

The first reading, 1 Corinthians 15: 20-28, contains these words: 'Christ is indeed raised from the dead, the first fruits of those who have fallen asleep... Christ must reign until God has put all enemies under his feet, and the last the enemies is death.' After the reading of Psalm 23 the gospel followed, John 12: 23-26: 'The hour has come for the Son of Man to be glorified... Unless the grain of wheat falls to the earth and dies, it remains only a grain. But if it dies, it bears much fruit...'

In his homily Archbishop Romero spoke of the departed lady's simple faith, and said: 'You have heard in Christ's gospel that one must not love oneself so much as to avoid getting involved in the risks of life that history demands of us, and that those who try to fend off the danger will lose their lives. But whoever out of love for Christ gives themselves to the service of others will live, like the grain of wheat that dies, but only apparently. If it does not die, it would remain alone... Only in undoing itself does it produce the harvest...

"...The expectation off a new earth must not weaken but rather stimulate our concern for cultivating this one. For here grows the body of a new human family, a body which even now is able to give some kind of foreshadowing of the new age... That kingdom is already present in mystery. When the Lord returns, it will be brought into full flower..."[89]

This Holy Mass, this Eucharist, is an act of faith. With Christian faith we know that at this moment the wheaten host is changed into the body of the Lord, who offered himself for the world's redemption, and in this chalice the wine is transformed into the blood that was the price of salvation. Many this body immolated and this blood sacrificed for humans nourish us also, so that we may give our body and blood to suffering and to pain - like Christ, not for self, but to teach justice and peace to our people. So let us join together intimately in faith and hope at this moment of prayer for Doña Sarita and ourselves.'

Murdered

Just after these words the tapes of the Mass record a gunshot. From the door at the back a single gunman fired point blank at the archbishop, who was behind the altar; he fell to the ground; the bullet had entered his left breast and was lodged in his back; he suffered heavy internal bleeding in his chest. He was quickly carried to a small truck which took him the five minutes' drive to the Policlínica hospital. In an emergency room there he continued to choke on his blood and died within a few minutes.

Onlookers reported that the killer drove away under the protection of police cars[90]. Subsequent investigations linked the killing to Major Roberto D'Aubisson, the founder of the political grouping ARENA, which now plays a leading role in the government of El Salvador. The country reacted with horror to the killing - schools were closed, days of mourning and strike were proclaimed, and even Romero's opponents joined in expressing condolences[91], as did countless people all over the world. Oscar Romero's Funeral Mass the following Sunday, Palm Sunday, reflected the extent to which he was loved by the people, the worsening violence in the country and the abiding divisions among the bishops. In the days leading up to the funeral a group of the faithful began a fast in the cathedral and hung up a banner saying that most of the bishops (who were named) the Secretary of the Bishops' Conference and the American Ambassador should stay away: they did.[92]

Funeral

It is thought at about 200,000 people did attend the Mass, set up outside the cathedral, including a large number of priests and bishops from all over the world. Pope John Paul II was represented by the Mexican Cardinal Ernesto Corripio. Tragically during the cardinal's homily a bomb exploded in one corner of the piazza and shooting broke out, probably from the National Palace. Amid the chaos that ensued Romero's body was rushed into the cathedral, along with thousands of people - it was hastily buried in the east transept and the Mass was never finished. Outside the cathedral thousands fled and forty people were killed in the stampede. The government issued a false statement about what had happened which was quickly contradicted by many of the bishops and foreign representatives - the violence had been initiated by the security services.[93]

Three years later John Paul II came to El Salvador. On 8th March 1983 he broke off from his planned itinerary to go and pray at the tomb in the cathedral and he referred to Oscar Romero as 'The zealous pastor who was led by love of God and service to his brothers to the supreme sacrifice of his life in a violent way while celebrating the sacrament of forgiveness and reconciliation'

Romero is a good modern example of how popular devotion to those whose lives were marked by heroic sanctity often breaks out long before formal beatification and canonisation, as he is venerated all over Latin America, with shrines to him in countless homes, especially the homes of the poor. In these pages we have reflected on his life and teachings as part of the process the Church is undertaking of discerning the will of God. These closing words are a poem by Bishop Pedro Casaldáliga CMF:

'Saint Romero of the Americas,
Our shepherd and our martyr
No one shall ever silence
Your last homily.'

Further Reading

Romero, Oscar, *The Violence of Love,* compiled and tr. J. R. Brockman SJ, San Francisco: Harper and Row 1988.
- *The Church is All of You*, compiled and tr. J. R. Brockman SJ, London: Collins 1985.
- *A Shepherd's Diary*, tr. by I. B. Hodgson, London: CAFOD and CIIR 1993.
- *Voice of the Voiceless: The Four Pastoral Letters and Other Statements,* tr. M. J. Walsh, Maryknoll, NY: Orbis 1985.

Brockman, James R., SJ, *Romero - A Life* revised edition Maryknoll, NY: Orbis, 1989. The first edition was published in 1982.
- *The Spiritual Journey of Oscar Romero*, *Spirituality Today* vol. 42 no. 4 (Winter 1990), pp. 303-322, available online at *http://www.spiritualitytoday.org/spir2day/904242brock.html*

Lopez Vigil, María, *Oscar Romero - Memories in Mosaic,* London: CAFOD and DLT, 2000.

Hayes, Michael A. and Tombs, David *Truth and Memory - The Church and Human Rights in El Salvador and Guatemala,* Leominster: Gracewing 2001.

Pelton, Robert S., CSC, *Monsignor Romero - Bishop for the Third Millennium*, Notre Dame, Indiana: University of Notre Dame Press 2004.

Pope Paul VI Encyclical Letter *Populorum Progressio* (1967) CTS Do 273
- Apostolic Exhortation *Evangelii Nuntiandi* (1975) CTS S 312.

Pontifical Council for Justice and Peace *Compendium of the Social Doctrine of the Church,* London: Continuum 2005 (Original, *Libreria Editrice Vaticana* 2004).

Cavanaugh, William T., *Torture and Eucharist*, Oxford: Blackwell, 1998.

Irene B. Hodgson (ed.) *Through the Year with Oscar Romero* (London: DLT/CAFOD 2006)

Sobrino, Jon SJ:
   Archbishop Romero - Memories and Reflections Maryknoll: Orbis 1990.
   A Spirituality of Liberation, Maryknoll, NY: Orbis 1988.

Chittister, Joan OSB, *A Passion for Life - Fragments of the Face of God* Maryknoll: Orbis 1996, pp.100ff.

Eaton, May Eaton *Authority and the Role of Archbishop Oscar A. Romero in the Struggle for the Liberation of the Salvadoran People* San Salvador: Guayanopopo, 1994.

Gearon, Liam, *A Modern Martyr: the story of Oscar Romero*, Norwich: Religious and Moral Education Press 1998.

Video

Romero, starring Raúl Julia and directed by John Duigan, Warner Home Video 1989 (distributed by St Paul Multimedia productions). While the film takes liberties with incidents and chronology and changes the names of many characters (including most of the bishops) Julia's presentation of Romero's personality is very powerful. The hatred towards him on the part of the political Right and the rich is captured vividly.

The Archbishop Romero Trust

While there are a number of research initiatives in Latin America and the USA dedicated to Oscar Romero's life and teachings, the foundation in 2005 of the Archbishop Romero Trust is the most important step taken in this country to hallow his memory. Details of the foundation's work can be found on *http://www.romerotrust.org.uk/*. The five patrons are the Cardinal Archbishops of Westminster and St Andrews and Edinburgh, the Archbishop of Dublin and the Anglican Archbishops of Canterbury and York.

Endnotes

[1] When the Archdiocese of San Salvador initiated the process of beatification and canonization Pope John Paul II gave Romero the title 'Servant of God' as is customary in these cases (for details of the process see *http://romeroes.com/canonizacion/canonizacion.html*).

[2] 9th May 2007: the interview is reproduced in full on the Vatican website, *www.vatican.va* – follow the links to the visit to Brazil for the Fifth CELAM assembly. It is striking that twice the Holy Father uses the term 'witness' which is the basic meaning of the word 'martyr'. He went on to say 'The problem was that a political party wrongly wished to use him as their badge, as an emblematic figure. How can we shed light on his person in the right way and protect it from these attempts to

exploit it? This is the problem. It is under examination and I await confidently what the Congregation for the Causes of Saints will have to say on the matter.' Earlier on he says that he had been given an important new biography: this is *Primero Dios*, by Professor Roberto Morozzo della Rocca (2005). It is sometimes claimed that the references to Romero in the interview were deleted in Vatican press releases.

[3] Encyclical letter *Fides et Ratio* (1998, CTS Do 654), 43, quoted by Cardinal Oscar Rodriguez Maradiaga SDB, 'Monsignor Romero' in Robert S. Pelton CSC *Monsignor Romero - A Bishop for the Third Millennium* (Notre Dame, Indiana: University of Notre Dame Press 2004), p.24.

[4] The address on this occasion was given by Fr Michael Campbell-Johnson SJ, Martyrdom and Resurrection in Latin America Today: Archbishop Oscar Arnulfo Romero, published in Michael A. Hayes and David Tombs (eds.) *Truth and Memory - The Church and Human Rights in El Salvador and Guatemala* (Leominster: Gracewing 2001), pp.44ff.

[5] See in particular the document from the Sacred Congregation for the Doctrine of the Faith, Instruction *Libertatis Conscientia* (1986), 68, quoted in *Catechism of the Catholic Church* 2448.

[6] See Hayes and Tombs, *op.cit.*, especially chapters 1, 3, 6 and 7.

[7] See Mary Grey, A Theology for the Bearers of Dangerous Memory and Dermot A. Lane, Memory in the Service of Reconciliation and Hope in Hayes and Tombs, *op.cit.*, pp.161ff.

[8] See on this William T. Cavanaugh, *Torture and Eucharist* (Oxford: Blackwell 1998).

[9] *Romero - A Life* (Maryknoll: Orbis 1989), a revised version of the earlier *Oscar Romero - Bishop and Martyr* (1982).

[10] Archbishop Luciano Mendez de Almeida SJ, Martyrs, Heroes and the Contemporary Church in Pelton, *op.cit.*, p. 31.

[11] In Spanish speaking countries a person's mother's surname to be added to the father's in the full form of a name.

[12] All these details from Romero's childhood are from material gathered from friends and relatives, published in section one of María Lopez Vigil, *Oscar Romero - Memories in Mosaic* (CAFOD and Darton, Longman and Todd, 2000).

[13] *Reflections by Zaida Romero, ibid*

[14] Described in *ibid.*, pp. 17-18.

[15] Ruben Zamora, The Enflowering Spirit of Archbishop Romero in Pelton, *op.cit.*, p. 47.

[16] See on this *Shepherd of Sheep and Wolves* in Lopez Vigil, *op.cit.*, pp.21ff.

[17] 10th July 1965, quoted by Rodriguez in Pelton, *op.cit.* p. 18.

[18] Nelly Rodriguez in Lopez Vigil, *op.cit.*, p. 22.

[19] Brockman, *op.cit.*, p.40.

[20] For example his speech of 2nd October 1962 in which he said 'There is a third enlightening point – the Church, in the presence of peoples on the way to development, discovers what it is and what it should be: the Church of the poor, that is the Church of everyone' quoted by Bishop Samuel Ruiz Garcia, 'Monsignor Oscar A. Romero' in Pelton, *op.cit.*, p. 72.

[21] Document 14, *Poverty of the Church*, 1 and 2, quoted by Ruiz, p.73. The bishops at Medellín also taught: 'If "development is the new name of peace" (Pope Paul VI, *Populorum Progressio*) the Latin American underdevelopment, with particular characteristics of the different countries, is an unjust situation promoting tensions that conspire against peace…In speaking of a situation of injustice, we refer to these realities that express a situation of sin.' (Document 2, Peace) and again, 'Christ, our Savour, not only loved the poor but rather "being rich he became poor"; he lived in poverty; he centred his mission on the announcement to the poor of their liberty and he founded his Church as a sign of that poverty among people…The present situation demands, therefore, of bishops, priests, religious and the laity, the spirit of poverty which "breaking the bonds of selfish production of material goods, stimulates the Christian to organically dispose the economy and power toward the benefit of the community" (Pope Paul VI, *Address at the Mass for the Day of Development*, Bogotá, 23rd August 1968). The poverty of the Church and of her members in Latin America should be sign and commitment – sign of the immeasurable value of the poor in the eyes of God, and commitment to solidarity with those who suffer.' (Document 14, *Poverty of the Church*, 7, quoted by Ruiz, with more examples).

[22] *Ibid.*, p. 19.

[23] Dean Brackley SJ, *Rutilio and Romero*, in Pelton, *op.cit.*, p.82.

[24] *Ibid.*, pp. 82-83.

[25] Lopez Vigil, *op.cit.*, pp. 50ff.

[26] Quoted by Rodr\iguez in Pelton, *op.cit.* p.5

[27] Lopez Vigil, *op.cit.*, pp. 47ff.

[28] Pelton, *op.cit.*, Introduction, p. 6

[29] 'The Church must cry out by command of God. God has meant the earth and all it contains for the use of the whole human race. Created

wealth should reach all in just form, under the aegis of justice and accompanied by charity... It saddens and concerns us to see the selfishness with which means and dispositions are found to nullify the just wage of the harvesters. How we would wish that the joy of this rain of rubies and all the harvests of the earth would not be darkened by the tragic sentence of the Bible: "Behold, the day wage of labourers that cut your fields defrauded by you is crying out, and the cries of the reapers have reached the ears of the Lord." [James 5:4]' quoted by Pelton, *op.cit.*, p. 7.

[30] *Ibid.*, p. 6.

[31] *Evangelii Nuntiandi* (CTS S 312) section 31. This document is often viewed as the most important document the Church has ever issued on evangelisation and made an immense difference to the Church's approach to missionary activity all over the world. See P. Hebblethwaite, *Paul VI - The First Modern Pope* (London: HarperCollins 1993) pp. 651ff.

[32] Brockman, *op.cit.* p. 8.

[33] *Op.cit.*; this was the title of the first chapter of the book in the earlier (1982) edition of the autobiography; it is *The New Pilot* in the 1990 edition.

[34] *op.cit.*, p. 9. Some children to whom they gave a lift in their car ran off.

[35] See Brockman, *op.cit.*, pp.15-17 for an account of exchanges between Romero and Gerada.

[36] Jon Sobrino SJ *Archbishop Romero Memories and Reflections* (Maryknoll: Orbis 1990), p.19

[37] Brockman, *op.cit.*, p. 20.

[38] As happened when the President's brother was murdered in September 1979.

[39] One might be surprised because throughout Latin America military chaplains, and the military vicars (such as Bishop Eduardo Alvarez in El Salvador) were often strong supporters of the military and of military governments.

[40] The first reading at the Mass was Zechariah 12:10-11.

[41] Extracts in Brockman, *op.cit.* p. 62 -63 and Romero *The Violence of Love* (San Francisco: Harper Row 1988); the full text (in Spanish) is in R. Cardenal, I. Martin-Baro and J. Sobrino (eds.) *La Voz de la Sin Voz: La Palabra Viva de Monseñor Romero* (San Salvador: UCA Editores, 1980), pp.207ff.

[42] Later in 1977 in the village of Osicala.

72

⁴³ For these see Margaret Hebblethwaite, *Base Christian Communities and Small is Beautiful...*

⁴⁴ Picture in Brockman, *op.cit.*, following p. 174.

⁴⁵ *Ibid.*, p. 154.

⁴⁶ Roberto Cuellar, *Monseñor Oscar Romero: Human Rights Apostle* in Pelton, *op.cit.*, p. 45.

⁴⁷ *Ibid.* p. 36.

⁴⁸ Sobrino, *op.cit.*, pp. 35ff. shows how he criticized analytically some of the positions of the political Left.

⁴⁹ Oscar Romero, *A Shepherd's Diary* (tr. Irene B. Hodgson, London: CAFOD/CIIR 1993), pp. 133 – 155 and Brockman, *op.cit.*, pp. 157 – 163. For a summary of CELAM III's teachings see Rodger Charles SJ, *Christian Social Witness and Teaching*, volume 2 (Leominster: Gracewing 1998), pp. 269-282.

⁵⁰ See Cavanaugh, *op.cit.*, especially on the united decision of the bishops of Chile to excommunicate those involved in torture, probably including Pinochet himself, pp. 253ff.

⁵¹ This is an example from the *A Shepherd's Diary*: 'The bishops' meeting at the nunciature confirmed the division among us. We could agree only on officially denouncing the assassination of Father Macías...when we tried to look at the causes, the meeting was dominated by the prejudice that there is Marxist infiltration in the Church. It was impossible to overcome that prejudice, in spite of my trying to explain that many priests are persecuted because they want to be faithful to the spirit of Vatican II, translated for Latin America by Medellín and Puebla. This was understood very little. Rather, the blame was laid on the instruments of Marxism which, according to them, the Church is serving. I offered this test of my patience to God, since I was being blamed in great part for the evil occurring in the country and in our Church.' (p. 306) See also the account of the elections of officers for the Episcopal conference in November 1979 in Brockman, *op.cit.*, pp. 206ff.

⁵² According to Brockman (*op.cit.*, p. 126) Romero had suggested this but 'Bishop Aparicio was not interested.'

⁵³ These included the priests Romero used as his advisers, his relationship with his new auxiliary Bishop Revelo and the length of the archbishop's homilies.

⁵⁴ Quoted in the *A Shepherd's Diary* p.69.

[55] Brockman, *op.cit.*, pp. 177-180, gives details of the document, entitled *Political-Religious Situation in El Salvador*, attacking Romero, the Jesuits, priests who had been killed and the church radio station.

[56] Of Francisco Coll, a Dominican who had founded the Dominican Sisters of the Annunciation, a congregation which had several schools in San Salvador, who had invited Romero to be their guest at the ceremony.

[57] *A Shepherd's Diary* p.215.

[58] *Ibid.*, p. 466-7.

[59] See on this Cavanaugh, *op.cit.*, chapter 1, 'Torture and Disappearance as an Ecclesiological Problem'. Romero did seek advice from Cardinal Raúl Silva, Archbishop of Santiago, about the workings of the diocesan *Vicaría de Solidaridad* which did so much to support victims of torture and violence and acted as a centre of opposition to General Pinochet's regime (Cuellar, *op.cit.*, p.45)

[60] At various times the cathedral was occupied by groups of workers or opponents of the regime, so cathedral Masses were transferred to other churches in the city.

[61] Quoted in Brockman, *op.cit.*, p. 5. Six priests were assassinated during Romero's time as archbishop: Rutilio Grande SJ (12.3.77), Alfonso Navarro Oviedo (11.5.77), Ernesto Barrera (28.11.78), Octavio Ortiz Luna (20.1.79), Rafael Palacios (20.6.79) and Alirio Napoleon Macías (4.8.79; he was a priest not of the San Salvador archdiocese but of the diocese of San Vicente, presided over by Romero's adversary Bishop Pedro Aparicio: for his ambivalent response to his death see Brockman, pp. 182-3).

[62] For a fuller summary see Brockman, *op.cit.*, pp. 22-24.

[63] For a fuller summary see Brockman, *op.cit.*, pp. 80-84 and Rodriguez, in Pelton, *op.cit.*.

[64] *Archbishop Romero and His Commitment to the Church* in Pelton, *op.cit.*, p. 54.

[65] CTS Do 680.

[66] Drawing on Blessed John XXIII's encyclical *Pacem in Terris* (CTS S 264) and Vatican II's Pastoral Constitution on the Church in the Modern World, *Gaudium et Spes* (CTS Do 724), paragraph 11, the letter calls the popular organizations 'signs of God's presence and purposes.'

[67] Quoting Paul VI, *Evangelii Nuntiandi* 37.

[68] 'Of evident and prolonged tyranny that seriously attacks the fundamental rights of the person and dangerously harms the common

good of the country', Encyclical letter *Populorum Progressio* (1967, CTS Do 273), 31.

[69] For a full summary see Brockman, pp. 138-144.

[70] See Campbell-Johnson in Hayes and Tombs, *op.cit.*, pp. 54ff

[71] The letter quotes the Puebla *Message to the Peoples of Latin America*, no.3.

[72] For a summary of the fourth pastoral see Brockman, pp.187 – 195. On all the pastorals see also Campbell-Johnson in Hayes and Tombs, *op.cit.*, pp. 44ff. and Rodriguez and Swedish in Pelton, *op.cit.*, pp. 15ff. and 51ff. The letters are gathered together with other statements in the collection *Voice of the Voiceless* cited above in the bibliography.

[73] Described in Brockman, *op.cit.*, p.234: '...he was not accessible enough, let himself be overwhelmed with problems, was irascible, inconsistent in the way he received others, causing fear in those who did not know him. He could give sharp answers that humiliated others. All this they attributed not to character defect but to his not sharing with others the burden of the heavy problems that he had to bear.'

[74] *Ibid.*, p. 51.

[75] In Hayes and Tombs, *op.cit.*, p. 51.

[76] This is another example from a sermon: 'If we truly believe that Christ, in the Eucharist of our Church, is the living bread that feeds the world, and that, as a believing Christian who receives this Host, I am the instrument, then I should bring in it into the world. I have the responsibility of being the leavening of society, of transforming such an ugly world. This, yes, would change the face of our country, to truly inject the life of Christ into our society, in our laws, in our policies, in all our relationships. Who is going to do this? You are! If all of you, the Salvadoran Christians, don't do this, then don't expect El Salvador to be fixed. El Salvador will only be leavened with divine life if the Christians of El Salvador truly propose not to live a lazy faith, a fearful faith, rather truly as the saint – I think it was Saint John Chrysostom – said, "When you take communion, you take Communion, you receive fire." You ought to leave breathing joy, with the strength to transform the world.' Irene B. Hodgson (ed.) *Through the Year with Oscar Romero* (London: DLT/CAFOD 2006), pp. 47ff.

[77] Quoted in James R. Brockman SJ, *The Spiritual Journey of Oscar Romero*, Spirituality Today vol. 42, no.4 (Winter 1990), pp. 303-322, available online at *http://www.spiritualitytoday.org/spir2day/*

904242brock.html. The article gives the most comprehensive picture of Romero's spiritual development and examines his psychological state.

[78] He wrote in 1940: 'This is your heritage, O priest: the cross. And this is your mission: to portion out the cross. Bearer of pardon and peace, the priest runs to the bed of the dying, and a cross in his hand is the key that opens the heavens and closes the abyss.' (*Ibid.*, p. 2)

[79] Brockman, *Romero - A Life*, p. 27.

[80] *Ibid.*, p. 41.

[81] *Ibid.*, p. 233.

[82] In England and Wales, for example, the 'gutter' end of the Catholic press delights in attacking the bishops and trying unsuccessfully to drive a wedge between them and the pope.

[83] Brockman, *op.cit.*, pp. 230-231.

[84] *Ibid.*, pp. 232-233.

[85] He criticised acts of violence committed by groups occupying the cathedral (such as the torture and injury of a policeman, at this time) but felt he needed to negotiate with them (Brockman, pp.240ff. and elsewhere).

[86] For a summary see Brockman pp. 240ff. and extracts in *The Violence of Love*.

[87] *Ibid.*, pp. 241-242.

[88] He was editor of the newspaper, *El Independiente*, whose offices had been bombed a week before.

[89] Here Romero quotes *Gaudium et Spes*, 39.

[90] See Brockman, Appendix, 'Romero's Killers', pp. 249ff.

[91] Although the television and radio stations controlled by the oligarchy 'continued their programmes as if nothing had happened.' (Brockman, p. 245)

[92] Bishop Aparicio had come to view the body in the cathedral, amid hostile remarks. Of the Salvadoran bishops only Rivera was present at the funeral. Unsuccessful efforts were made by the archdiocesan authorities to get the banner removed.

[93] For details see Brockman p. 247.

Informative Catholic Reading

We hope that you have enjoyed reading this booklet.

If you would like to find out more about CTS booklets - we'll send you our free information pack and catalogue.

Please send us your details:

Name ....

Address ....

....

....

Postcode..

Telephone...

Email ....

Send to: CTS, 40-46 Harleyford Road,
            Vauxhall, London
            SE11 5AY

Tel: 020 7640 0042
Fax: 020 7640 0046
Email: info@cts-online.org.uk